WHY PAIN?

WHY DOES GOD ALLOW PAIN AND SUFFERING?

EVANS FRANCIS

ISBN 979-888555107-6

Contents

Introduction

Why does God allow pain and suffering in some form or the other in our lives? Everyone has asked God this question at some point because we all experience pain physically, emotionally, socially, mentally, and financially. Any one of these painful encounters can be traumatic and result in worry, depression, frustration, confusion, loneliness, and negative thoughts. But did you know pain leads to maturity and growth in your Christian life? In fact, to achieve anything in your life, you must learn to endure pain, for without it you cannot mature.

In those painful seasons, always remember in the garden of sorrow, Jesus suffered for you. He took the crown of thorns on His head and became our sacrificial Lamb for slaughter. He was bruised and crushed and finally nailed on the cross. That was the highest demonstration of love for us. The pain you go through cannot be compared to the hurt and humiliation Jesus endured. He was led to Calvary with the thorns on His head, carrying all the bruises and stripes on His body. Without any fault, He was cruelly nailed to the cross. He did it silently without complaint and became our Saviour, Redeemer, Deliverer, victorious Lord and, above all, the Lamb of God without blemish.

When we stand in the same place, our problems dissipate at the revelation that Jesus conquered death. The same resurrected Christ will lead you to a new path, to a new resurrection.

This inspiring book will draw your attention to real-life experiences, trials, hardships, and tragedies that are part of the human condition. It will also share how we can overcome these sufferings to come out triumphantly. As you read, you will receive a revelation of the great wonders and truths of God's promises.

Each one of us is born with a purpose according to God's will, which we must faithfully pursue and live out. I pray you will find hope, courage, and strength to face all the adversities of life and you will come out of trials victoriously in Christ. Stay blessed. Shalom.

Connect with Evans Francis

WhatsApp: https://wa.me/919960877313

YouTube: www.youtube.com/evansfrancis

Facebook: https://www.facebook.com/evansfrancis831

Instagram: https://www.instagram.com/evansfrancis831

Website: www.evansfrancis.org
www.evansfrancisbooks.com
www.christianappdevelopers.com

Email: contact@evansfrancis.org

CHAPTER ONE

PAIN AND YOU

Why must we undergo pain? Why does God allow it in the first place? What did I do to deserve this? Why? Why? Why? The answer would surprise you. God is using pain to prepare you for greatness. How does gold become precious and valuable? When it is refined by hot, burning fire. You cannot purify gold without heating it but when it comes out of the fiery process, we receive it in its purest form. It is impossible to get pure gold without putting it in the fire. In the same way, God uses pain in our lives (fire) to make us people of value.

Pain is inevitable and cannot be shared with anyone. The person who is suffering has to bear it alone. It is an integral part of life and cannot be avoided. However, we must learn how to live with it and be victorious through it.

The first time I ever thought about writing on pain was on December 5, 2011, when I suffered a life-threatening accident. An Indica car ran over me at a speed of 70 km/h, injuring me from head to toe. This accident has completely changed my perspective on life.

Sickness was no stranger to me because I spent around 70 percent of my life in hospitals living on medication. I wondered why it was all happening to me. All sorts of questions were popping up. The most painful thing was when I was judged by people saying God was angry with me, and He was teaching me a lesson. They concluded I was living in sin and made many accusations. I felt condemned. But when I started to go through the Scriptures, I found a totally different outlook. It was here I received hope and understanding that God does not allow us to go through pain to break us. On the contrary, it is to prepare us for something bigger.

At the hospital, I counted the number of times I had suffered pain in so many ways. It started when I was seven months old and continued throughout my youth right up until today. I am now twenty-four. At that time, I viewed pain as a curse but today, I can say it is a blessing. Today, I understand all the pain was for my good and whatever I am today, everything I do today, my character, attitude, love for the poor, destitute, and others, everything is the outcome of the pain I went through.

God tells us in Hosea 4:6, "My people are being destroyed because they don't know me." Many people are destroying themselves because they do not have the knowledge of the Word of God. But I guarantee you after reading this book, your personal perception of pain will totally and permanently change.

When the Holy Spirit inspired me to write on pain, and I shared it with some of my loved ones, I did not get positive responses. Some people may even oppose the title of this book. They consider pain a curse. You see, everyone likes good health, success, and prosperity but run away from pain, suffering, and failure. This is a sign of immaturity.

During our lives, we all have at least one role model, someone we desire to be like, but we do not want to endure the pain he/she had. A person whose dream is to become a bodybuilder can never achieve his goal if he does not accept the pain of exercise. It seems the more pain you give your body, the more muscle you build. You can never get a certificate in anything without passing an exam. In the same way, God allows pain to mould and train you so you can become a useful vessel.

Apostle Paul compares this moulding to a lump of clay, "Has not the potter power over the clay, of the same lump to make one vessel unto honour, and another unto dishonour?"(Romans 9:21 KJV).A lump of ordinary clay is chosen by the potter from the shapeless pile of clay heaped on the floor. The potter has an end product in mind, a vessel that will be useful for its final purpose. The potter labours over the clay, forming and shaping it until the final product is realised. Then the pot can be fired and embellished.

Without the process of kneading, moulding, and going through the fire, the pot can never become a useful vessel. Before meeting the firing process, it is fragile and weak; it cannot hold even a little amount of water. But when it has finally gone through the fire (pain) process, the material that emerges is tough, resilient, very close to stone, which can contain almost anything. While the clay is still pliable and wet, the great potter's desire is to make a work, not just for utility but also beauty out of that which is otherwise marred, flawed, and unsuited for His use. The potter heats the pot to the point the clay is matured. Likewise, God, the Potter, allows us to go through the fire to cause us to mature.

Can you imagine a mere clay pot complaining to the potter? Does the pot have rights of its own? No, it exists for service as the potter intended it. In the same way, we have no right to ask God why? Only He knows how much strength we need to face the challenges in the future. Before the clay was baked, it was not fit for anything, but after it was baked in the fire, the finished vessel could be used.

The clay cooperates with the potter and goes through the pain, knowing whatever the potter does will give it value. Similarly, we must cooperate with God. Avoiding pain does not accomplish anything; it will only make you a man or woman of compromise. If you compromise your faith, there is no place for you in the kingdom of God.

James 1:2-4 tells us about the value of suffering:

Dear brothers and sisters, when troubles of any kind come your way, consider it an opportunity for great joy. For you know that when your faith is tested, your endurance has a chance to grow. So let it grow, for when your endurance is fully developed, you will be perfect and complete, needing nothing.

The preceding verse says consider pain an opportunity for growth. So be joyful, delighted, and happy when you fall into all sorts of trials, problems, and pains. Why? Because the testing of your faith produces endurance, which is patience. When you are patient in your time of testing, it will make you perfect and complete, lacking nothing.

There are people who will tell you that you are suffering because of your father's or grandfather's misdeeds. That is utter rubbish and a lie. Read Ezekiel Chapter 18. There is no such thing as a generational curse. This is all man-made stuff. Jesus Himself became a curse for us, as it is written in Galatians 3:13:

But Christ has rescued us from the curse pronounced by the law. When he was hung on the cross, he took upon himself the curse for our wrongdoing. For it is written in the Scriptures, 'Cursed is everyone who is hung on a tree.

Others may tell you it is because of your own sins, but I will say, if you are going to heaven, it is only because of what Christ has done for you. God loves us, not because of who we are but who He is. I personally believe if God allowed you to suffer that pain, He has a plan and purpose for you in that too.

And we know that God causes everything to work together for the good of those who love God and are called according to his purpose for them. (Romans 8:28)

Don't think your self-righteous deeds will merit blessings:

All our righteous acts are like filthy rags. (Isaiah 64:6 NIV)

There is no one righteous, not even one. (Romans 3:10)

Let no one deceive you in any way. (2 Thessalonians 2:3 NIV)

Today, when I see or think about the pain I went through, I consider it a blessing. Earlier, I used to view it as a curse, but today, I understand God was preparing me for a bigger work. Today, when I meet people in pain, poor and without clothes, I know how they feel because I have gone through it. Some people will tell you if you do not have a home, you are cursed. They forget our forefathers in Christ who died in jungles and villages without owning anything just for the sake of the gospel.

If owning a home was a blessing, Jesus would have been born in a palace. Jesus told us in Luke 9:58, "Foxes have dens and the birds in the sky have nests, but the Son of Man has no place to lay his head."

Ephesians 4:14 warns us not to be like immature children being deceived by every doctrine and teaching.

Then we will no longer be immature like children. We won't be tossed and blown about by every wind of new teaching. We will not be influenced when people try to trick us with lies so clever they sound like the truth.

But how can we do this? Ephesians 5:11 goes on to tell us

Take no part in the worthless deeds of evil and darkness; instead, expose them.

Exposing the unfruitful works of darkness is what I do, and no one likes it. You may ask me then, what should we do? The Bible gives the answer in Acts 17:11: we should be like the Jews at Berea. What did they do? These Jews were more open-minded than those in Thessalonica, for they eagerly received the message. They were more willing to learn, examining the Scriptures daily. They did not accept everything they heard; on the contrary, they very carefully examined what they were told and what they heard to see whether Paul and Silas were telling the truth.

I will never tell you to believe what I write blindly; instead, take out your Bible and compare it with the living Word of God. Only if it aligns with the Word should you accept it. But this time, you have no excuse to reject it. Jesus already warned that many would come to deceive us. It is in our hands to decide whether we should allow anyone to trick us or to check what the

Word of God tells us to do. God has set His Word as a boundary beyond which no Christian should go. If it is not in the Bible, it is not meant for us.

Remember, pain is not meant to destroy. Rather, it builds a Christ-like character in you, which will help you to grow in Christ's likeness until your last breath. So, accept your pain and glorify God as you go through it. Remember, there is no gain without pain.

CHAPTER TWO

How Can Pain Glorify God?

You cannot escape pain. It is not a matter of whether it will come into your life or happen to someone very close to you; rather, it is a matter of when and how much. You are either coming out of one storm or heading into another.

God sometimes allows us to go through pain, suffering, or trials so His name is glorified. You may say it is not possible because that is not the nature of God. God is good; He can never do this. Let's see what Romans 9:14-18 says:

Are we saying, then, that God was unfair? Of course not! For God said to Moses, "I will show mercy to anyone I choose, and I will show compassion to anyone I choose." So, it is God who decides to show mercy. We can neither choose it nor work for it. For the Scriptures say that God told Pharaoh, "I have appointed you for the very purpose of displaying my power in you and to spread my fame throughout the earth." So, you see, God chooses to show mercy to some, and he chooses to harden the hearts of others so they refuse to listen.

Do you think God could not have helped the Israelites to leave Egypt after the first plague? Why did He let them go through all ten? Of course, He could have removed them. But did He? No. Why? Only to demonstrate His power through which His name could be glorified. How God delivered the Israelites from each of the ten plagues was a miracle, but God had more to show. The parting of the Red Sea was the final miracle to show God's marvellous hand on those He wanted to deliver and His judgement on those He wanted to punish. Hardening Pharaoh's heart was part of the process.

Today, if I meet any person or I go to any place to share the gospel, it is easy for me to preach because many receive Jesus by hearing my testimony. When I share about the pain I went through and how God miraculously healed me, kept me alive, and is using me for the work of His kingdom, that itself is enough for anyone to understand the God I preach about is the living God.

If we look at the life of Daniel and his friends, we see God allowed them to go through severe trials to test whether they would reject Him or face a life-threatening punishment.

Daniel's Friends Are Tested

In Daniel Chapter 3, we read about Daniel's friends Shadrach, Meshach, and Abednego, who had been brought to King Nebuchadnezzar's court as slaves when the Babylonians invaded Jerusalem.

King Nebuchadnezzar had made a huge, golden statue of himself and set it up in the plain of Dura. He called all his officials to the dedication of the statue, giving the order to everybody that as soon as they heard the musical instruments playing, they had to bow down to the statue. If anyone should disobey the order, they would be thrown into a blazing furnace.

All the officials obeyed the king's order and bowed down to the statue. But Shadrach, Meshach, and Abednego did not bow down. Do you know why? Because there was a higher law, God's law, which specifically commanded they should neither make nor bow down to idols:

You must not make for yourself an idol of any kind or an image of anything in the heavens or on the earth or in the sea. (Exodus 20:4)

Their disobedience was reported to the king, and they were summoned to his presence. The king offered them a chance to reconsider their decision. However, the three young men replied to the king:

O Nebuchadnezzar, we do not need to defend ourselves before you. If we are thrown into the blazing furnace, the God whom we serve is able to save us. He will rescue us from your power, Your Majesty. But even if he doesn't, we want to make it clear to you, Your Majesty, that we will never serve your gods or worship the gold statue you have set up. (Daniel 3:16-18)

I want you to notice the total commitment of the three men to their God. Even though the king was giving them a chance to save themselves and recant, they stood firm. They believed in their God to rescue them but even if He did not, they would never bow down to other gods. Their faith was deeply rooted in honouring their God, whatever the cost.

On hearing their declaration, the king's face turned red with anger. He ordered the men to heat the furnace seven times hotter than usual and commanded strong soldiers to tie up Shadrach, Meshach, and Abednego and throw them into the furnace. It was so hot the men who escorted the three young men were instantly killed by the leaping flames.

God Delivers His Servants

But Shadrach, Meshach, and Abednego were not harmed by the fire. The king saw them walking in the fire unbound and unharmed. He also saw a fourth man walking with them, who looked like the Son of God. It was the Lord Himself.

Then the king called out to them, and they came out. On examining them, they saw the fire had neither harmed their bodies nor was a hair of their heads singed. Their clothes were not scorched, and there was no smell of fire on them. Then Nebuchadnezzar made a decree:

Praise to the God of Shadrach, Meshach, and Abednego! He sent his angel to rescue his servants who trusted in him. They defied the king's command and were willing to die rather than serve or worship any god except their own God. Therefore, I make this decree: If any people, whatever their race or nation or language, speak a word against the God of Shadrach, Meshach, and Abednego, they will be torn limb from limb, and their houses will be turned into heaps of rubble. There is no other god who can rescue like this!" Then Nebuchadnezzar promoted Shadrach, Meshach, and Abednego to even higher positions in the province of Babylon. (Daniel 3:28-30)

Daniel in the Lions' Den

Daniel was thrown into the lions' den because he refused to cease praying to his God rather than pray to the Persian Emperor. You will find the whole story in Daniel Chapter 6.

King Darius the Mede decided to divide the kingdom into 120 provinces each ruled by a high officer. HeThe king also chose Daniel and two others as administrators to supervise the high officers and protect his interests.Daniel soon proved himself more capable than all the other administrators, and the king made plans to place him over the entire empire.

These officers were jealous of Daniel and began searching for some fault in the way he was handling government affairs, but they couldn't find anything. Their only chance of accusing Daniel would be in connection with his faith, so they went to the king with this proposition:

Long live King Darius! We are all in agreement—we administrators, officials, high officers, advisers, and governors—that the king should make a law that will be strictly enforced. Give orders that for **the next thirty days** any person who prays to anyone, divine or human—except to you, Your Majesty—will be thrown into the den of lions. And now, Your Majesty, issue and sign this law so it cannot be changed, an official law of the Medes and Persians that cannot be revoked." So, King Darius signed the law (Daniel 6:6-9, emphasis added).

Note that Daniel could have talked himself into obeying the law and cease his praying in public for a season. After all, it was only thirty days! Then he could go back to his normal practice and everything would be resolved. But that would be a compromise: it would put the law above his God. See what he did next:

But when Daniel learned that the law had been signed, he went home and knelt down as usual in his upstairs room, with its windows open toward Jerusalem. He prayed three times a day, just as he had always done, giving thanks to his God.

Then the officials went together to Daniel's house and found him praying and asking for God's help...Then they told the king, "That man Daniel, one of the captives from Judah, is ignoring you and your law. He still prays to his God three times a day" (Daniel 6:10, 13).

The king was deeply troubled, and he tried to think of a way to save Daniel. But he could not change the order he had just signed. So, at last, he gave orders for Daniel to be thrown into the lions' den. "May your God, whom you serve so faithfully, rescue you," was all he could say.

Then the king returned to his palace troubled; he couldn't sleep at all that night.

Let's continue to read this amazing story from Daniel Chapter 6:

God Delivers Daniel

Very early the next morning, the king got up and hurried out to the lions' den. When he got there, he called out in anguish, "Daniel, servant of the living God! Was your God, whom you serve so faithfully, able to rescue you from the lions?"

Daniel answered, "Long live the king! My God sent his angel to shut the lions' mouths so that they would not hurt me, for I have been found innocent in his sight. And I have not wronged you, Your Majesty."

The king was overjoyed and ordered that Daniel be lifted from the den. Not a scratch was found on him, for he had trusted in his God.

Then the king gave orders to arrest the men who had maliciously accused Daniel. He had them thrown into the lions' den, along with their wives and children. The lions leaped on them and tore them apart before they even hit the floor of the den.

Then King Darius sent this message to the people of every race and nation and language throughout the world:

"Peace and prosperity to you!

"I decree that everyone throughout my kingdom should tremble with fear before the God of Daniel.

For he is the living God,

and he will endure forever.

His kingdom will never be destroyed,

and his rule will never end.

He rescues and saves his people;

he performs miraculous signs and wonders

in the heavens and on earth.

He has rescued Daniel

from the power of the lions."

So, Daniel prospered during the reign of Darius and the reign of Cyrus the Persian. (Daniel 6:19-28)

Daniel knew his God and, as he later would say, the *people* who *know their God shall* be strong and carry out *great exploits (Daniel 11:32)*. He had committed no offence; yet, he was condemned to die like a criminal. But God miraculously saved him. At the end, who received the glory? God Himself. Many times you face problems, not because of your wrongdoing, but God allows them to come into your life so His name can be glorified. With God, all things are possible.

Let's revisit the last line of both stories:

Then Nebuchadnezzar promoted Shadrach, Meshach, and Abednego to even higher positions in the province of Babylon. (Daniel 3:30)

So, this Daniel prospered during the reign of Darius and the reign of Cyrus the Persian. (Daniel 6:28)

They stood firm in their faith and did not complain during the hour of temptation but trusted in the living God. Therefore, you can see how God blessed and honoured all four of them before men.

We read John Chapter 11 about how Lazarus was raised from the dead. When Jesus came to know His good friend was sick, He said this sickness was for the glorification of God. In the four Gospels, we can see Jesus ever willing to reach out to the sick and even the dead, for example, Jairus' daughter and the widow of Naim's son. However, in the case of Lazarus, Jesus deliberately delayed His visit by four days, so that through the amazing miracle, God's name would be glorified. Jesus turned around that tragic death into life. God can work now as He did with Daniel, his friends, and Lazarus. He knows the right time, and in His time, He makes all things beautiful.

You too may be going through a serious problem, which you feel you do not deserve. But I want to tell you, my beloved brother or sister, allow God to do His work and when it is done, you will be astonished at His hand over you.

...

You are rich when you are content, whether you are blessed or facing a crisis. Learn to trust God no matter what. No worldly fire or lion, not even death itself, can harm you if you trust God and let Him work through you. Your Creator will always keep you safe and His name will be glorified for the expansion of His kingdom.

CHAPTER THREE

HIDDEN PLANS BEHIND THE PAIN

I strongly believe this book will help you to find answers to many of your questions related to pain and also encourage you as you go through it. In this chapter, I want to throw some light on what the hidden plan is behind the pain that enters our lives.

Praise be to the God and Father of our Lord Jesus Christ, the Father of compassion and the God of all comfort, who comforts us in all our troubles, so that we can comfort those in any trouble with the comfort we ourselves receive from God. For just as we share abundantly in the sufferings of Christ, so also our comfort abounds through Christ. (2 Corinthians 1:3-5 NIV)

Many a time when we go through pain and suffering, we think it serves no purpose. We murmur and question God, but God allows it to happen for a higher purpose. He desires to teach us several things, which will be beneficial to many who are going through the same situation. Can you ever imagine a virgin girl telling a woman in labour she can understand the mother's pain? No! She has never been through it. God knows the kind of trials and tribulations we experience will be of great help in building the lives of others. And having been through pain, we can empathize and help others in similar situations.

Always remember, our God knows our past, present, and future. Everything in our lives is valuable to Him. Jesus tells us:

What is the price of two sparrows—one copper coin? But not a single sparrow can fall to the ground without your Father knowing it. And the very hairs on your head are all numbered. So don't be afraid; you are more valuable to God than a whole flock of sparrow. (Matthew 10:29-31)

If the little sparrows are valuable to God, how much more are we in His sight—even the hairs on our heads are counted. Do you think He will do anything to hurt us? Never, my friend. Always remember, God sacrificed His only begotten Son for you and me; that is the extent of His love for us. Whatever He allows in our lives, He has a good purpose behind it.

Recently, I met a mother who had lost her new-born daughter. I could see the pain she was going through but still, she shared that she wanted to help mothers with new-born babies who are in danger of dying without proper care. Today, she has started a society, which totally works for new-born babies. Yes, she lost her daughter, but with that pain, God is using her to touch many mothers who would have lost their new-borns without help. The pain she went through made her understand the pain many families go through, and she decided to work for such people only. Pain and suffering can help us comfort others who are going through similar hurt.

Many orphanages, welfare organizations and NGOs are the beneficiaries of the founders' decision to make a difference in society. Today, if this book helps you in any way, it is only because God allowed me to go through pain so I could be a blessing to many who are sitting in hopeless situations. Even if anyone calls me in the middle of the night to come to their home because someone is in pain, I rush to them. I know what pain is all about. I know very well what a person lying on a hospital bed feels. That is why I love to visit hospitals and old age homes because there are people who have no one to talk to and need to be prayed for.

Our Troubles Are Light Compared with the Glory

That is why we never give up. Though our bodies are dying, our spirits are being renewed every day. For our present troubles are small and won't last very long. Yet they produce for us a glory that vastly outweighs them and will last forever! So, we don't look at the troubles we can see now; rather, we fix our gaze on things that cannot be seen. For the things we see now will soon be gone, but the things we cannot see will last forever. (2 Corinthians 4:16-18)

The apostle Paul wrote that our suffering is "light" and "momentary" compared to the "eternal glory" that will be our reward. Yes, beloved, the physical pain we go through is nothing when compared to that glory. Many people try to live here happily and forget about their eternity with God. Always remember how we live here on the earth determines our future with Jesus Christ. Scripture tells us in Matthew 10:28:

Don't be afraid of those who want to kill your body; they cannot touch your soul. Fear only God, who can destroy both soul and body in hell.

Why Did Job Have to Suffer?

I am certain the book of Job was written for one main purpose: to illustrate what happens when we go through pain, suffering, and trials. Job was a righteous, God-fearing man. However, Satan wanted to take the glory from God by showing that Job was only righteous because God had blessed him with a large family and many possessions. He wanted to show that Job's faith was conditional upon God blessing him. To prove his point, Satan approached God's throne and asked God's permission to bring hardship upon Job to see if he would curse God. God allowed this, so Job was stripped of his sons and daughters and his possessions. Despite all the pain, Job still worshipped God.

Satan went back to God and asked to attack Job directly. God said he could, as long as he didn't take Job's life. Job was afflicted with boils and was in great pain to the extent his wife told him to curse God. His friends repeatedly tried to convince Job his difficulty was a result of unrepented sins—with friends like them, who needs enemies? They were of the mindset godly living brings blessing, and ungodly living brings curses.

Job cried out to God, but there was no answer. Finally, after what seemed like forever, God responded by reminding Job of all His creation, power, majesty, and wonder. Awe-struck, Job responded with these words:

I had only heard about you before, but now I have seen you with my own eyes. I take back everything I said, and I sit in dust and ashes to show my repentance. (Job 42:5-6)

Job realised God was all-powerful, he was not. His job was to believe God was in control, and He could be trusted. In the end, God was merciful to Job and blessed him more in his latter days than his earlier days.

Just imagine the Bible without the book of Job. Suppose Job had not gone through the pain and suffering, his example would not be there to give hope to many in similar pain. Always remember our God is in control all the time. Often, pain and suffering can help to shape our personalities.

The Danger of Pride

Many times, God allows pain to prevent us from becoming self-righteous. God hates the proud and over-spiritual. Paul said his "thorn in the flesh" was to keep him from becoming proud and arrogant.

So, to keep me from becoming proud, I was given a thorn in my flesh, a messenger from Satan to torment me and keep me from becoming proud.

Three different times I begged the Lord to take it away. Each time he said, "My grace is all you need. My power works best in weakness." So now I am glad to boast about my weaknesses, so that the power of Christ can work through me. That's why I take pleasure in my weaknesses, and in the insults, hardships, persecutions, and troubles that I suffer for Christ. For when I am weak, then I am strong. (2 Corinthians 12:7-10)

God's grace is sufficient for us to overcome any pain and suffering in our lives. Secondly, He will never allow us to go through the pain we can't handle. As written in 1 Corinthians 10:13:

No trial has overtaken you that is not faced by others. And God is faithful: He will not let you be tried beyond what you are able to bear, but with the trial will also provide a way out so that you may be able to endure it. (NET)

Sometimes, pain and suffering in the life of one person can result in the advancement of the gospel in the life of another. I had a burn mark on my left hand after the road accident, and that mark itself opened new opportunities to share the gospel to many.

I want you to know, brothers and sisters, that my situation has actually turned out to advance the gospel: The whole imperial guard and everyone else knows that I am in prison for the sake of Christ, and most of the brothers and sisters, having confidence in the Lord because of my imprisonment, now more than ever dare to speak the word fearlessly. (Philippians 1:12-14 NET)

I know of many families and people who accepted Christ because of the problems they were facing, and they saw Jesus working in their situation. As apostle Paul said, his imprisonment had, in fact, helped to advance the gospel.

Always remember, beloved, whatever you are going through, nothing is hidden from God. Nothing happens in our lives without His knowledge. Keep your eyes on the Lord, as He never takes His eyes off you. No matter the severity or depth of the pain, He is sufficient for you to overcome and be victorious to glorify His name.

CHAPTER FOUR

MY TESTIMONY

For to me, to live is Christ and to die is gain. (Philippians 1:21 NIV)

Dear friends, I hope this book has greatly blessed you. As I am nearing the end of writing it, I feel a bit sad to be leaving you. But I believe it has helped change your life to make you realise your true value. My reason for writing this book was never to earn money or fame but to reach out to you. I know it is not possible for me to reach each one of you personally but where I cannot, this book can.

I now wish to share my testimony with you. I hope this will encourage you, help you change your focus, and bring you closer to God.

I started doing God's work at the age of nineteen—all glory and honour to God! Without His help, I would not have gone anywhere or accomplished anything in my life. Whatever I am today is because of two reasons: God's grace and I was never bothered about what people thought of me. I did what God told me to do. When God tells you to do something, He does not often show a clear path. I was never afraid to trust in Him and unquestioningly did what He told me. Today, I would have been amongst the dead, buried somewhere. However, it's only because of the grace and unending love of Christ that I am alive and sharing my testimony with you.

I am an evangelist working in God's vineyard for the expansion of His kingdom. I come from Nagpur, India. I was born in a very small town, Mukerian, in Punjab on February 24, 1988. God blessed my parents with children at the cost of giving them to Him for His work. My parents were faithful to that promise and likewise, God blessed them with three children whom they dedicated long before their birth. I have two older sisters.

Before I was even conceived, my mother had a vision of a little baby fully naked standing in front of her. It was God's sign that her next child would be a boy. My mother shared this vision with my father and they surrendered themselves to God's plan. My mom suffered while carrying me, and the Devil tried his utmost to destroy me in the womb itself. But the Lord never allowed it to happen, as is written in Psalm 112:10, "The desire of the wicked shall perish" (NKJV).

At six months old, I had a high fever and two attacks of fits the very same day. That subsided but at eight months, again, I had a high fever and had five attacks in a single day. At the advice of the family friends, my parents took me to the Christian Medical College in Ludhiana where I underwent treatment for epilepsy for five years. During treatment, I never had any attacks again. With the fervent prayers of my family and friends, I recovered. I am a living witness to God's Word: "For nothing will be impossible with God" (Luke 1:37 NET).

My most vivid recollection of my childhood was being constantly sick. For example, if I played, I would have pain in my legs, so I was not allowed to play much. In short, my family had to take care of me all the time. The Devil tried his best to end my life many times through sickness, but my God always miraculously healed me and kept me alive to testify to those who didn't believe in God. Since my childhood, I have always loved to care for those who were oppressed and in pain. Somehow, the feeling came naturally to me.

I always knew God had a plan for me, but long before I could recognise it, I fell into bad company. I mixed with friends who did not know Jesus, and they led me away from the godly life I was called to. In that season, I enjoyed their company so much I forgot God. I forgot my calling. I forgot everything. I was totally caught up in the things of the world. I even forgot Jesus died for me. Even though I used to call myself a Christian, I was not a true believer. I was proof that calling oneself a Christian doesn't make you a born-again believer. The people of Antioch gave the name "Christian" to the followers of Christ because they could clearly see Jesus Christ in them through their attitudes, behaviours, and characters.

During this time, I had reached the ninth standard. One day, suddenly, I had a stomach-ache. I thought it was normal pain, but it wasn't. The pain kept growing every minute until it was unbearable. Even now when I think about it, tears come to my eyes at the intensity of the pain I felt. It lasted for three days. I vomited more than fifty times a day. In that agonizing pain, crying and rolling in bed, I gave my life back to Jesus. I told Him, "If You give me one more chance and forgive all my sins, I will live for You until my last breath." By around 9:00 p.m., my condition had deteriorated, and I was taken to the hospital. I could barely walk; I was literally crawling.

I was admitted and immediately put on intravenous drips. I can never forget the feeling of being so light when I got the first intravenous treatment and the pain subsided. The next day, I got ultrasounds, x-rays, and various other tests. The doctor said I needed to undergo surgery, but the cost was too much for my family to handle. My dad asked the doctor to treat me with medication for three days. If nothing happened, then we would think about the surgery. The doctor diagnosed my condition as acute pancreatitis, a very rare condition that occurs in alcoholics, but we have no family history of alcohol abuse.

The doctor also said if there had to be surgery, it would be major, and the chance of survival was very low as I had come to the hospital quite late. My family, friends, and partners in Christ prayed for me. After three days, the doctors examined me again. To their surprise, I was a lot better and responding well to the medication.

I was kept without food or water for five days and after eight days, I was discharged from hospital. Later, I found out some people had even fasted and prayed for my recovery too. My healing was the result of those fervent prayers and tears. In short, I will say God pulled me out of the ocean of sin and is now using me to win souls for His kingdom.

Since my childhood, I have always loved people who are in need and in pain because I know what pain means. I always used to wonder how I could make a difference in the lives of such people. All glory and honour to God—today, He is doing that through me. No matter how small or big, each act is for Him and Him alone. By God's grace, we are running an NGO named TWCO, that is, Together We Can Organization. The motto is "Let's live for others." This motto was greatly inspired by the Lord Jesus Christ. He came on this earth for sinners like you and me. He lived and cared for others who were sick, rejected, dejected, and hated by society. He carried our sins and sickness and gave His life for us.

There is an urgent need to do the work. By the time you read my testimony many would have gone to hell, and we would have done nothing about it. It's time for action as is written in James 1:22, "Be ye doers of the word, not hearers only" (KJV). I never sit at home wasting time. I see to it that I preach the gospel to at least one person a day. By God's grace, wherever God has sent me to date, I have seen His power manifest in signs and wonders in the lives of people. It is not because of me or who am. It is God in His graciousness who is using me to touch those troubled souls.

As the Bible teaches, Jesus is a deliverer, and He uses me as an instrument to deliver others. Praise the Lord! Our ministry team visits hospitals, orphanages, old age homes, and helps them out of our limited resources. Helping the servants of God, providing food, and clothing to the sick, and praying for the sick is our biggest priority.

Pure and undefiled religion before God and the Father is this: to visit orphans and widows in their trouble and to keep oneself unspotted from the world. (James 1:27 NKJV)

On May 1, 2011, we started our God-given first church named House of Deliverance at Nagpur. This is a place where we pray for the sick, demon-possessed, and troubled. I always say I am a believer, not a beggar because I preach Jehovah-Jireh who provides all our needs according to His riches in glory, not ours. It's easy to preach but practising what you preach is more important. Ephesians 6:8 tells us, what we do for others, God will do for us.

When God told me to start this ministry, I had no money in my account but miraculously, He supplied all our needs. I truly believe when the body of Christ stands together, we can shake the nations. The only reason for working so hard in my youth is I have a deep passion to save the lost. It pains me to see people perishing in their sins and heading toward eternal condemnation.

Today, my heart aches when I look at many youngsters. They think they are enjoying their lives but do not realise it's at the cost of their eternal destiny, and they are moving one step closer to hell with each passing day.

Many think if they believe in Jesus, they have passports to heaven. But the truth is, beloved, you must make your life count for Christ.

Don't you realize that friendship with the world makes you an enemy of God? (James 4:4)

No one can serve two masters. (Matthew 6:24)

Don't copy the behavior and customs of this world. (Romans 12:2)

A clear warning is given in the above verses not to follow the ways of the world.

As a pig loves to play in the mud, today's generation love to play with sin, not knowing what they are going into. Recently, we started a group named God's Brigade whose vision is to see youth living for Christ. Our mission is to motivate, equip, and mobilize them to pull down enemy strongholds. My real motive is to teach people who they are in Christ and what God desires them to be. I am not here on this earth to build my kingdom, which many are doing; it's only about God's kingdom.

God created man in His own image, but we have become puppets in the hands of the puppet master, the Devil. People don't like me because I tell the truth, but I'll continue nevertheless! Man has not called me or is providing for me. God is. I would rather live to be a God-pleaser than a man-pleaser because no man died for me; only Jesus did!

I encourage you, my brothers and sisters in Christ, if God can use someone like me, a backslider at one point, God can use anyone. When I was in my final year of school, I never passed a single progress test. My friends used to say I would fail but when I did my final examination trusting God, I passed miraculously. It is all about God's grace. From the beginning, I've been repeating only one thing and that is "God's grace."

Friends, this is my true and living testimony. I'm here only for God and will do so all the days of my life because I have only one desire: when I meet Christ, I hear from my Saviour these precious words, "Well done, good and faithful servant!"

My Deliverance

I will not die; instead, I will live to tell what the LORD has done. (Psalm 118:1)

On December 5, 2011, I was involved in an accident near my home. The front shock absorber of my two-wheeler broke, and I fell on the road. A high-speed car that was tailgating me rammed into me. The car ran over half my body; the front wheel of the car ran over my left shoulder. I was stuck under the car. The driver panicked and reversed. Then he went forward dragging me along with the car. This resulted in my shoulder getting dislocated and I suffered multiple abrasions, starting from the back of the head, shoulder, waist, hands, up to the knees.

While I was in the hospital, I saw four circles glittering and hovering over me. I felt in my spirit those were the angels sent by God to protect me. The Holy Spirit inspired me with a verse from Psalm 34:20, and I claimed it, "For the Lord protects the bones of the righteous; not one of them is broken!" Even though I had felt and heard the distinct sound of the cracking of the bones in my ribs and shoulder, the x-ray showed no broken bones, only dislocation. This is the proof of the miracle my bones were protected by the angels. I completely believe, along with my friends, relatives, and well-wishers, my bones were made flexible like rubber.

In addition, I received burns from the hot engine on my left arm and left cheek near the eye, which resulted in 1.5 inches of multiple deep wounds. I was taken to the emergency centre and later shifted to a hospital.

Miraculously, I was discharged after only three days. It was a miracle I survived this massive accident, having been hit by a vehicle driving at approximately 70 km/hr.

Had it not been for God's grace, I do not know what would have happened to me. Friends, this is God's grace, which I have been talking about since the beginning. Two weeks before the accident, I was praying around 2.00 in the morning, I was lying down and suddenly, I went into a trance. I saw myself driving and a car ran over me, Then I came out of a coma after three days.

Immediately I called one of my uncles and he told me it was nothing. It was just a dream; nothing would happen to me. I too forgot it but when my vehicle's shock absorber broke and I fell to the ground, I remembered God had already shown it to me. I was about to faint but suddenly, I remembered if I fainted, I would go into a coma.

When I was discharged, I was mad at God. I asked Him, "Why, why, why?" After three days I got the answer for my testimony. God never allows suffering to break us, beloved, but to make us, mould us, and shape us into vessels He desires. God showed me two weeks prior to this His motive was that I should not go into a coma, although He allowed the accident to happen. When we go through crises, we are angry, but later, we realise there was a higher purpose to it. People were surprised to know I was discharged from the hospital after three days and completely recovered in a month, up and about, driving and running around to do God's work.

Recently the doctors told me I had a kidney stone, which the sonography confirmed. We prayed and then I went to have another sonography. Believe it or not, the stone was gone! Jesus Himself removed it. Nothing is impossible for our Lord and Saviour Jesus Christ.

Jeremiah 29:11 assures us that God has a good plan and purpose for all of us. And that includes you. The decision is yours whether to choose God who leads you to eternal life or the world, which leads you to eternal condemnation. Always remember we are all sinners and Jesus Christ is the only answer to our sins. Only through Him can you truly know and experience God's grace, redemption, and perfect plan for your life.

Jesus said in John 14:6, "I am the way, the truth, and the life. No one can come to the Father except through me." You need to understand one thing here. Jesus never said Mary and Me or Joseph and Me. He said, "I am the way." No one else!

Dear friends, I was rejected by everyone, but I remember the Word of God, "The stone that the builders rejected has now become the cornerstone" (Psalm 118:22). This is what Jesus does when He takes control of our lives. It is only possible when we give our lives to Him and ask Him to be the Master of our lives. Always remember if Jesus is in your boat of life, it can never sink.

Beloved, I always say the following:

- Living is for Jesus.
- Dying means going to Him.
- Every heart that beats belongs to Him.
- Every breath is for His praise.
- If all live for themselves, why can't I live for others?

Beloved, I started God's work at the age of nineteen and up to now, God has never allowed me to be ashamed. On the contrary, I have earned the respect of others. Today, wherever people call me to minister, I go. If it's God's will, I'll surely come to your city too and to your homes, if you invite me. Remember one thing: alone I can't, but together we can share the gospel and see our nation worshipping the living God, Jesus Christ, our Lord and Saviour in spirit and in truth.

May God be with you and bless you. Remember me and our God-given ministry in your precious prayers.

Stay blessed!

Shalom!

CHAPTER FIVE

INSPIRED MESSAGE

In this chapter, whatever the Holy Spirit inspires me to say, I will write. Do not read it with a critic's mindset but with a learning heart. I am a man of foolish words. I am weak in narration, but whatever I am today is all because of God's grace. I have nothing to boast about other than Christ died for me, and all I dream about is to live for Him and Him alone.

I want you to read the following Scripture.

Jesus told them this story: "A man had two sons. The younger son told his father, 'I want my share of your estate now before you die.' So, his father agreed to divide his wealth between his sons.

A few days later this younger son packed all his belongings and moved to a distant land, and there he wasted all his money in wild living. About the time his money ran out, a great famine swept over the land, and he began to starve. He persuaded a local farmer to hire him, and the man sent him into his fields to feed the pigs. The young man became so hungry that even the pods he was feeding the pigs looked good to him. But no one gave him anything. (Luke 15:11-16)

In the preceding passage of Scripture, we can see a son who is demanding his share of the inheritance from his own dad. Many times in our lives, beloved, we do the same thing. We dictate to God, "I want this. I want that" without even bothering to ask, "Does He really want me to have it?" Many times, we desire small things, not realising more is due to us than we could ever imagine. So, just like this son, many of us have made decisions that suit our personal whims without even caring what our heavenly Father thinks.

God allows us to make our own choices just as He allowed Adam and Eve to make the wrong choice. Their decision to sin brought suffering and chaos to the whole world. Sinful desires carry spiritual consequences, including

God's judgement. In our daily lives, it is the small choices that add up to the big choices, which will determine our future.

This son decided to leave his father to enjoy his life. Many of us leave Jesus just to have a good time. Many of us think we would never have betrayed Jesus like Judas Iscariot and hand Him over to the Romans. But I want to tell you, friend, whenever you compromise with Jesus, you are standing in the same place where Judas once was. Judas accepted 30 silver coins to hand over Jesus to the Romans. Would you skip your prayer time, church services, quiet time, and everything for those you met yesterday and not the One who bled and died on that cross until His last drop of blood was shed?

Initially, sin can be exciting, enjoyable, and cool, but we do not understand we are getting into big trouble. That son was enjoying life and suddenly, the famine struck. It happened only after he had spent everything. Many times, when we enjoy sin, we think it is fabulous, but after losing everything—our future, our education, the will of God—the problems mount up. When the Prodigal was destitute, all his so-called friends left him. No one was left to stand by him. How lonely he must have felt, realising there was no one to love him, care for him, or support him.

Why did this have to happen? Who was responsible for the mess? It was the Prodigal's decision alone. Proverbs 3:5 tells us, "Trust in the Lord with all your heart; do not depend on your own understanding." I come across many people in tears because of the situation they have landed themselves in, not because of their parents or family, but because of their own intellectual reasoning, which has no place for God.

The Prodigal's one wrong decision led him to a life of having to eat pig's food to survive. What a pathetic condition. Can we blame God? No. Why? Because the Prodigal exercised his free will. He made the choice to follow a certain lifestyle. Of course, his father must have tried to dissuade him but, at the end of the day, he decided what he wanted to do. We cannot blame God for the consequences of our poor choices. He gave His all for us—His only begotten Son. But it is in our hands to decide if we need Him or not. We decide whether to depend on God to protect us or not.

Many are angry with God for the wrong things happening in their lives. Maybe you are too, but dear brother and sister, it is your decision that is the root cause of all your problems. I encourage you, instead of blaming God, accept the mistakes you made. He is ready to forgive you and the best thing about Him is when He forgives, He forgets.

And I will forgive their wickedness, and I will never again remember their sins. (Jeremiah 31:34)

I will never again remember their sins and lawless deeds. (Hebrews 10:17)

Let's go back to the prodigal story as Jesus tells it.

When he finally came to his senses, he said to himself, 'At home even the hired servants have food enough to spare, and here I am dying of hunger! I will go home to my father and say, Father, I have sinned against both heaven and you, and I am no longer worthy of being called your son. Please take me on as a hired servant.'

"So he returned home to his father. And while he was still a long way off, his father saw him coming. Filled with love and compassion, he ran to his son, embraced him, and kissed him. His son said to him, 'Father, I have sinned against both heaven and you, and I am no longer worthy of being called your son.'

"But his father said to the servants, 'Quick! Bring the finest robe in the house and put it on him. Get a ring for his finger and sandals for his feet. And kill the calf we have been fattening. We must celebrate with a feast, for this son of mine was dead and has now returned to life. He was lost, but now he is found.' So, the party began. (Luke 15:17-24)

It is written, "When he finally came to his senses." We need to do the same. We must realise our mistakes and make sound decisions. The Prodigal made the right decision to return home and apologise. And what was the outcome? His father forgave him and welcomed him back; they rejoiced together. Heaven rejoices over you when you come back to your heavenly Father, beloved. Luke 15:10 says, "There is joy in the presence of God's angels when even one sinner repents."

Many times, we end up in pain and suffering because of our foolish decisions. But when we give our failures to Jesus, He will help us and lead us to places we never thought of. You have read my testimony. Once I was in the ocean of sin, but when I allowed God to work, He made all things beautiful in His time.

I am a living testimony that if we give our all to God, He is enough to make our lives worth living. A person who spends time on his knees praying to God will never have difficulty standing on his feet throughout his life. I have suffered a lot of pain because of my wrong decisions. But I am encouraged by those whom God used in the Bible. They were not perfect; they were also ordinary people like us, and they too messed up. They too had conflicts just like we do. If God could use them, He can use us too. We are saved, not by what we do but by trusting what Christ has done for us.

Just imagine a life without pain and suffering. That would have limited our discovery. If we had not fallen sick, how would we have known God is a healer? If our friends and relatives had never left or abandoned us, how would we have known He never leaves or forsakes us? If we never felt sadness, how would we have known He is a comforter? If life was perfect, do you think we would ever search for God? Dear friends, we are fragile, but He is great, and He makes us strong.

Yes, friends, pain works as a pulley or a bridge, which draws us closer to God, and it is a proof we as humans have limitations. We may create many things, but He is the ultimate Creator. Doctors may perform an operation, stitch the wound, and pack up; but only God can heal.

Always remember, He stood in Gethsemane alone when all His disciples had left Him. He stayed on that cross, even though He could have come down anytime He wanted. Have you ever wondered what made Him go through such horrible pain? The answer is you and me. Jesus suffered pain for us so we can be healed (Isaiah 53:5).

It is an honour and privilege when I go through pain and suffering. I go through it with my Lord, experiencing His unfailing love. I am much encouraged by Revelation 3:21: "Those who are victorious will sit with me on my throne, just as I was victorious and sat with my Father on his throne."

As Jesus overcame all the trials and temptations of His life, when we walk with Jesus, He will surely help us to overcome all the obstacles. And as the Holy Spirit helped Jesus, He is there to help us too.

I believe this book has helped you in some way. I am not an author. Whatever the Holy Spirit inspired me to write, I have just written. This book belongs to God, and the author is Jesus.

All glory and honour to God alone!

Shalom!